Karen Hayes

THE HOUSES ALONG THE WALL

A Pembrokeshire poetry cycle

Holland Park Press London

Published by Holland Park Press 2018

Copyright © Karen Hayes 2018

First Edition

A CIP catalogue record for this book is
available from The British Library.

ISBN 978-1-907320-78-1

Cover designed by Reactive Graphics

Printed and bound by
CPI Group (UK) Ltd, Croydon CR0 4YY

www.hollandparkpress.co.uk

Karen Hayes created this cycle of poems as a fictional social landscape inspired by a row of houses along the coastal wall at the Parrog, near the small town of Newport in Pembrokeshire.

Each house appears in the poem with its actual name, whether in Welsh or English, but its history and inhabitants have been fictionalised and the details in the poems, although sometimes corresponding to a particular photograph or phrase, are entirely imaginary.

CONTENTS

Preface   9

Tesserae   13
In His Cups   15
The Last House on the River   17
Watermark   19
The Wedding Breakfast   21
Wax   23
Exposure   24
The Kayaks   26
The Ferryman   28
The Belgians   30
Fire on the Mountain   32
The Misses   35
Four Floors for Suzy   38
The Smell of Time   43
The Runt of the Litter   45
Congregation   47

Acknowledgements   49

PREFACE

What triggered the poems were the little pieces of pottery
which constantly wash up onto the beach at Newport
Sands. The beach underneath the wall, the Traeth Mawr
of the opening poem, is notable for the shards of broken
crockery that appear with each high tide. I could not
stop thinking about the households who had originally
drunk tea from the shattered cups and saucers and eaten
their dinners off the dislocated plates. Much of the local
art produced in and around this part of Pembrokeshire
incorporates these shards of pottery: they are like little
jewels, illuminations of other peoples' lives.

My children were very small at the time we first
visited this part of Pembrokeshire on holiday and it was
considered a great treat to rush out onto the mud after
each high tide and search for new fragments which were
hoarded, washed, stored and carried home in buckets and
water bottles.

We gradually began to invite other friends who also
had young families to come with us and to hire a house
to accommodate us all. There were around ten children
who all slept together in an upstairs dormitory and they
remember each stay as a return to their kingdom. The
children are all, with the exception of the youngest pair,
grown up now and so the dynamic has changed a bit and
our visits are not as regular.

The houses along the wall were gradually given over
to tourism during our time there and we became very
aware that the holiday house phenomenon was both
the thing that saved the area from falling into complete
disrepair but also what prevented the local population
from remaining in their home town, speaking Welsh in
the shops and claiming their own legacy. We were both

9

part of the problem and its solution. Talking to the local butcher, who was determined to keep Welsh lamb, reared on the welsh hills in his own shop even though the price of the meat meant that the only people who could afford to buy it were the English visitors, made me want to write about the simultaneous decay and preservation of a way of life, so I began to record not only what I saw along the sea wall but also what I imagined.

The stories told in the poems are a mixture of snippets of conversation overheard in shops, fragments of local myths and legends which occur in photos and journals in the houses, conversations in local pubs about incomers and economic exiles, the poignant story of the disappearance and presumed murder of Suzy Lamplugh and, above all the way that our own children all grew up together across almost twenty summers. In the midst of all these interests and concerns the original collection of china continued to grow.

The Houses Along the Wall also grew out of the urge to work in verbal and visual collage formats, creating a mythology from assorted fragments and impressions.

TESSERAE

Low tide turns midwife,
Delivering the river to the sea.
From silt the newborn samphire springs,
While further up the estuary
An egret clings to fish-rich tides
And hunts with leg in air.

Uncoloured Heron, lethal-eyed
Hangs upon the current.
Around the buoys, in half-buried seams
A rim of china lies
Where seagulls let them fall, inedible
And pattern side down.

Blue pigment, sometimes brown.
Leaves and petals, stripes and curlicues;
A red bird's beak with anxious eye,
An ink-green ship, a windmill blade.
Landscape turned hieroglyph.
In little pieces the mosaic is laid.

Such copious porcelain.
Its fractured stories interchangeable
On that unchanging shore.
Each plate and shattered cup
Rounded by meticulous sand
And put together again.

From Woolworth stores they came,
Or Jones and Higgins', slightly chipped,
Toby jugs and coronation mugs
And ashtrays from Ilfracombe.
Little bits of everyday, their shine gone off,
Lie dulling in the shallows.

If banquet sets could speak
What after-dinner speeches they would make!
What tea leaves read,
What secret things confide.
Contractions squeeze the water side
Where the heron stabs and kills.

The tales the washed-up china tells
Are scoured by the hard, heart-rinsing tide.

In His Cups

Morwellan

It was an affliction in the village;
Like polio or a stammer, it marked you out
As an object of sympathy.
Or pity rather... The sympathy
Was always for your wife
And she had been widowed by drink.
He had heard rumours
Passed coarsely amongst the men,
Vibrating between the women,
But in his cups he'd thought her beautiful.

Another man's wife; another's handprint
On her jaw. Her tears his bar.
Now though, as time is called for the long wait
In the stillroom, those fists have stiffened
And she has taken the pledge.
He watches her come out of the mission,
Clutched to the bosoms of female supporters.
Her shadow falls across the table
And into his pint of beer. It sours as
He gulps her down.

He watches her, moved by her spirit
Sunday by Sunday, walks the dry path
Down the long hill of her neck,
Lays parched at her throat's pool
Where a pulse will sometimes surface.
He's memorised that supple movement
With which she drops to her knees,
Drops with her, sweating behind his eyes.
He smells her tidal body like a malt flowing toward him,
In at the offertory, out at the creed.

15

His shilling, like ice in his palm, he touches
The rim of the collection bowl
Where the wood is warm from the heel
Of her hand and at the communion
Tastes where her lips have been.
And he knows how she gropes for the kneeler
Blindly with thumb and forefinger
And how she pulls
The resistant tapestry
Out of its hiding place.

She emerges from yew-tree dark
With the glamour of rain in her hair,
Her arm through his. Her smile an intoxication
To quench his thirst for ever,
And exacts her own promise in return.
He never took a drop from the day
She agreed to his proposal.
A Sunday it was. And wet. And he thought
How the church porch step was glistening
Like wine from the rock of God.

THE LAST HOUSE ON THE RIVER   *The Boat House*

This is the last house on the river,
      Tucked where an angle of mud resigns
      And where a remnant of the dun dune grass
      Shivers onto shore.

This is the place where limits overrun,
      Where earth and water inundate,
      Where river and sea embrace and separate,
      And then embrace again.

At this extremity the silver of water,
      The silver of sky and the silver of Heaven align,
      A tear at the edge of sight, a new horizon
      For the eye to journey in.

Let us lay down our marker,
      Where truth and time combine,
      Where inner and outer skin pucker the water,
      In slivers of our sudden seeming age.

Here, at the margent tide,
      Where pasts cannot be helped,
      Where futures are unfounded. The sound is
      Of my human heart, just under the sand,

Shell off, its frailties exposed.
      This moment, this now of terrible stillness,
      Between the wipe of the rain and the rubbing wind
      Debrided by the roar and holler

Of this day's breath on my skin.
    Where the waters meet and the wind is sweet in the mouth
    I calculate the dent my liberty leaves in air
    Against the weight of my shadow in the sun.

Last night you wore your favourite dress,
Its red nap turning plum
To sea-thread green.
You picked a path between the weed
At the foot of the harbour step,
And as the falling sun caught hold
You swung to brighter burnishes than gold;
A candle at water's lip.

Harsh as the clasp of shell on rock,
Stamped black upon the razor of the shore,
Defiant of tides,
Your step, a gasp which mingles
The insouciant cold of river
And the hungry cold of the sea.
The three of you, in spate, in shoal, in thrall
To a purpose I did not know you knew.

When you had crossed the waters, passed
The gleam of them on your body to dwindle to
Grey as lavender sand,
You were a whisper rolling in the Marram grass, unseen
And tiny as my hand.
I guess you must have lain full length
On the dune, in the dark,
Where the moon unpicked your seams.

This morning when you were not beside me,
When the river bowed afresh
To her partner, the sea,
The slow revealing margins of the land
Undrowned, were empty.
Now there is only the stain of you on my heart
And down on the beach a blowing hem,
The flag of your red dress.

THE WEDDING BREAKFAST   *Swyn y Mor*

From the recess of her window
She sees them gathering, like Gannets on a rock.
Perched in tiers upon each ledge,
Stockings swinging red or yellow or black
'Till every jag and spur holds twenty occupants.

Boatful by boatful, steered across the cwm,
Bows thickening the wrists of oarsmen ushers.
Flounced and be-frilled and topped with Sunday hats,
Swarming along the shelves,
The guests arrive.

Here the whole colony sit for the afternoon,
Passing clay bottles and jars of potted shrimp
And floral plates of Rees's crumbling welsh-cakes
Down the winding path of outstretched hands,
A human Ziggurat.

From her shadowed window
She watches the congregation sway for the toast.
Elbow to elbow, bride stitched to groom
And threaded like paper dolls. A double figure-head
Floats out to sea from the shallows of marriage.

At Swyn-y-Mor
She draws the nets that hang at her bedroom window,
Brief and brazen round her head, grey-veiled.
The ghost at the feast, a smudge at photo's edge.
A bride in all but ceremony.

One or two may have remembered
There had been talk of an understanding once,
But none of them look up.
The house of her heart, vacated long ago, is now
Shut up for demolition.

The wedding breakfast disappears,
In a swoop of seagull to cake crust.
The celebrations are complete,
Gannets skewer nuggets of bloated rice.
Her famine is their feast.

How many candles burned
In lighthouse miniature,
When one flame at the window
Was enough to tell a fisherman how far
He was from home. How far
From the wrecking rim of the bay,
How far from a bowl of broth
And the warming body locked around
His own, when you are cold and can only
Be warmed from inside.

How many candles flickered
On that out-breath of relief:
He's home, or dread: He's home,
Or disbelief: He's not.
The nine moons' turning darkness leave
A rocking cradle or an empty bed.
The fish pour from the nets,
Coal tipped in the scuttle for another week,
A step down to the stores for a slab of bacon on tick
And a pack of thin, white tapers.

How many candles shone
On nights identically black,
Each blessed in its paper wrapper,
Each hope confessed again.
And how many ears at the flaring pane
Awaiting the crunch of keel
And scrape of oars and the hefted nets and pots.
How that little light picks out a cigarette,
The glisten of spit on shingle, toe and heel,
Wet boots upon the beach.

Those buildings, dark as petrels in a storm,
Still cling to the sea wall.
Tenacious, webbed-foot houses built on rock,
Stare out toward their fortune.
In upper rooms their captains build sea-facing windows
And install telescopes trained to the oncoming weather.
The architecture here smells fresh as foresight:
Cargo matched to investment, fortunate crossings.
The sturdy science of commerce, reaching outward,
Beyond the mussel-pickers common-place
Of what to believe in, if not the promised land.

Those houses, high up on the Parrog,
Raise their three storeys to Heaven.
And squint at their gannet neighbours, lower down,
And almost within the crater of the harbour.
Hellish back areas emerge, where fish bins,
Slippery with guts, roll rotting.
Separate as topsail from keel, or officer from mate.
Down there they scrape the cargo
Of sand and twigs from their front doors,
As daily the sea hurls up its midden content,
And twice a year the equinoctial tides.

Those ships pull up as near as they can dare,
Laying at anchor in the dwindling pools,
Beached at midday, floating again by nightfall.
One, its whale-shaped hull full of coal,
Has its calf held tight by a rope to starboard,
Listing slightly and on the verge of extinction.
Pretending a future, caps pulled over eyes
In the light wind, a line of little cabin boys
Muster outside their houses along the wall
With harpoon sticks. Faces obscured,
They stand at attention looking out to sea.

THE KAYAKS

Craig-y-mor

At Craig-y-Mor the kayaks lean in rows
Watched by the owner from his sun-dried room,
And for a modest rental you can race them,
Singly or in convoy round the cwm.

Kayakers are the new breed on the Parrog,
Crowding the boat house bar, they block the light,
Their ostentatious wet suits smell of privilege;
Tourists are both a blessing and a blight.

As stealthy as egrets, landing once a year,
Weighed down with bargain booze and frozen clams
Purchased from stores in Cardiff or faraway London,
Bypassing the local price of hill-farmed lamb.

They come to practice dabbling in the sea,
To test the tides and flirt with water sports,
Unmindful of its life and death encounters,
Endurance as a pastime to be bought.

Three doors along, over a hump-backed path
The life boat station crouches on the cliff,
Its grey walls given over to luxury,
The imperatives of rescue cut adrift.

Its slipway mossy with stone-skimming children,
The wind carved men at the window, who watched the waves,
Have given way to stacks of cat-faced cushions
As if there never had been lives to save.

And as the path runs on to Bettwys Bach
A single life-ring hangs in public view,
Assurance, come wild weather or disaster
That substitutes the sturdy life boat crew.

Twelve pounds a day for a damp seat in a kayak,
A little armada, hitched to the incoming tide,
To skull with the sleek furred otters off the sand bank,
The swans like fierce, white gunboats alongside.

THE FERRYMAN

Bryn Alban

Jack Price the ferryman,
One penny to cross at low tide,
Tuppence at high.
His seven-decade skill can navigate
The changing skins of sand,
His practiced eye discerns
What swims beneath.
Noncommittal, pocketing the coppers,
Noticing who returns and who does not.

Two fares who cross
On the same days but never at one time,
Yet always come back together.
Jack watches them walk on the far side,
Cling to the contour of the dune,
And how, as the estuary reclaims them,
Clothing separates, his suit, her skirt,
A cuff extends to help her over a rock,
Jack sees the rouge of her, blushing in the sunset.

Neap tide, when the water
Barely troubles his boat,
A day whose stillness he'd remarked upon;
A white day, dark by five.
He'd only have taken a minute to collect the fare,
Untie the boat, release the oar, pass a good day.
But she won't wait. The silt flecks on her stockings,
Water wetting the hem of her dress,
She wades into the river.

She stumbles beyond his care,
Past the gulls which fling their gossip to the air,
Past the call of her mother on the jetty,
Past the clinging rim of the weed
And on to the further shore.
Jack sees her push through a current
Up to her heart, her heavy water mark,
And melt against the long form in the sand.
He thinks she will not be wanting to return.

Jack Price, unhitching his boat at dawn
Hears a rip in the air,
Turns his prow to the bold, new iron bridge
Where even the herons are not yet awake.
He catches the breath of her,
Catches her arc in the tail of his eye,
Her scrap of submerging colour.
And he thinks how she blends with the river
In the long sluice of her fall.

The Belgians came on the day of the regatta.
They flinched at the starting gun
And the press of supporters along the sea wall,
Unsettled by the whistles and flags
Of the partisan crowd.
They were amazed by our barbarian customs.
We also felt a kind of wonder,
Seeing that knot of children in the hallway
In their enormous hats,
With their anxious jibber jabber on the doorstep,
And a shadow behind them, wearing beads of jet:
That foreign woman must have been their mother.

You should be kind to them, said ours,
Extending an invitation to take tea,
And offering our riffraff services
To befriend the reluctant Belgies:
Teach them the tide times,
Teach them how to row,
And share our expertise at catching crabs.
They were not entirely on our side, it seemed,
But not against us either. That untranslated mother,
Who clearly loved her children too,
Wept at the melting sweetness
Of our proffered macaroons.

They had been overrun, the papers said.
We heard their tales of invasion
Like an absent history class and saw, in their shallows,
A fleet of Viking ships upon our beach.
At church I sat with Anneliese,
The shortest of the sisters,
Her hands all sticky with forbidden comfits.
I watched as the blotted, unfamiliar
Shape of a cross unfolded,
Smudged by podgy fingers
Onto her white pinafore.
And I noticed that she did not know our hymns.

Those three years, measured in regattas,
When the Belgians lived at Ocean House,
Marked an entente between us and next door.
On the last Sunday the eldest brothers won the double skulls
Then joined the fusiliers on Monday morning.
Their engraved cup still sits on our mantle-piece
With regimental medals from Palestine.
They spoke Welsh better than most boys in the village
And understood that we were the English here,
And therefore also foreign.
Amongst the list of Evanses and Reeses
Their Belgian name stands out.

FIRE ON THE MOUNTAIN   *Seagull Cottage*

From the garden
You cannot quite make out
The column of beaters.
Twig-figures busy on the mountain,
Insubstantial in the wavering air,
Though the bright line of their fire
Is clear enough.

Their beacons, pagan-hot,
Running along the frown line of Carn Ingli,
Salute in little eruptions,
As though the saint himself,
Walking the ridge,
Licked finger held aloft,
Blesses the wind's direction.

The day of the burning is
Never fixed in advance,
But arrives, like the landing of geese
At the edge of the spring,
With the land no longer drenched,
And the wind as dry as a kipper.
Arrives, like a sudden shiver.

The summons is conveyed
In the lift of an eyebrow,
A word or a shrug in the red-haired butchers,
A promise at milk-delivery,
A purpose in the spring of the sheep
And the running of the dogs a little faster
Home from the hill this evening.

Then up, up, up, men clamber,
Up to the stony ridges,
And scramble through the ferns
Which flinch at the thought of their own incineration.
Up to the balding cairn
To bare their voices
As the brand is put to the stalks.

Fire on the mountain.
Fire overtaking fire.
As the ancient army advances,
The sweat of it raw in the air,
The pyre of old growth, red as a dragon
Flaying that peak
Beneath the glossy sky.

The men still smell of flames
Long after midnight,
Loping along the cinder track.
One or two, those who misjudged the breeze,
Limp home a little singed,
Others are spangled by the lift and swallow
Of too many jugs of ale,

All bone tired,
All of them kings of the pyre,
Their linen stiff with smoke,
Their flesh anointed with grease and soot,
A crackle of light, torch bright behind the eyes,
Tongues raw with vapour,
Grass stalks ignite like tapers on the skin.

By morning the auto-da-fé
Is just a stutter underfoot
And the tang of scorch
And a charcoal-careless tapestry
Branded upon the oven of the earth.
Saint Brynnach's path is warm enough
To fry an egg for breakfast.

The kites fly lower today,
Sifting and sniffing for small casualties,
Plucking the burned little bones,
Like charnel treasure, off the mountainside.
Crows pick over the debris,
Undoing black lattices through which
The Spring already shoots.

THE MISSES   *Parrog House*

The first brick
Of the partition
Which will cut them loose
Is laid on a day in March,
Just as the early, pale primroses
Struggle from their green rosettes
And the highest tide of the year
Throws twigs right up
To the wrought iron gate which leads
To the soon-to-be-divided garden.

The last,
Which seals the Misses
Away from each other,
Is not cemented until May Eve.
And during the intervening weeks
A procession of relatives and friends
Arrives at their still single, grey front door.
Cousins in carriages, from Abergwaun,
Elderly aunts on foot from Newport Mountain.
Even their shared attorney-at-law,
Banging his badger-head walking stick
Free of the clotting sand,
Begging them not to proceed.

Anxious petitioners
File into their respective parlours,
Eyeing the Ormolu clock in one
And the grandfather in the other
And all the silverware,
Considerably devalued when
Declared as separate hoards.
They wait in identical sitting rooms
Each with its water colour view over the Parrog,
Or queue on parallel staircases
Whose treads rise slowly
Floor by floor,
Grasping the pale new plaster wash
On either side of the house.

Nobody counts the days beyond partition
Beside the misses themselves,
Who mark the weeks of liberation
On either side of the wall,
Circling month-minds, anniversaries
Of what has been undone, in miniature.
Head to head,
Immured in their separate single beds
They dream their nights in tandem
Returning in the dark
To the double path.

Tea is served at
Precisely ticking tea times
In respective halves
Of their mother's bone china tea set.
Each twin sits quivering
In their opposing parlours,
Each minus a milk jug or sugar bowl,
Nursing their grievances.
Once, the primary residence
On the thinning harbourside,
The house becomes two fiefdoms.
The village divides its loyalties,
Serving the misses whims
With flurries of separate deliveries
Timed not to coincide.

Sea Haven and Ocean View,
Two narrow paths,
Twinned arteries leaving the heart
Lead down to the single gate
Whose iron posts boast
A couple of mermaids in profile.
Two facets of the whole,
A pair of hemispheres,
Helen and Clytemnestra,
Like halves of an egg
And two identical queens rule over
Half a kingdom each.

FOUR FLOORS FOR SUZY   *Ondara House*

1

Our first floor
Lies close to the ground;
Pegged out, its corners stretched
Four square to the horizon.
This world is flat,
Constructed for day to day necessity.
Here we eat and squabble in the kitchen
And shit in the downstairs lav
And Suzy tells tales of abductions by the fire
Which spits its burning gobbets onto
The shabby carpet.

Down here, amongst the dead men
Are our hard won exits and entrances,
Where we run out to the shining sands,
Collect the windfall pears to feed to the gulls
Or loll on the bench with a forbidden fag.
From here we set out to hunt for foiled eggs;
Teams of children, Suzy in command,
Filling our makeshift baskets,
Unmindful of either death or resurrection.
This flat world, from where
We advance in hope of adventure
Is the same world to which we will return.

And when we make an appointment
Or decide what to cook or which book to read
Our decision has form.
It is the architecture of our will,
Whether to walk to Nevern
By way of the pilgrim cross
Or whether to climb Carn Ingli in a flurry of snow
And look for the fairy grotto,
Or whether to simply lie
Stretched flat on the dune and do nothing at all.
We have made decisions our refuge,
Made them in cubits of length and breadth
And so they become our truth.

2

Our second floor
Is the one which brings us to adulthood,
Mapping the reasoned roundness of the world
Like new discovered coastlines.
Here are the landings and the bedrooms
Where our sleeping parents lie,
Where they shut themselves away
To engage in their grown-up mysteries
And unspeakable acts,
Hissing at each other through mouthfuls of alcohol
Or lying on separate continents
Upon the ocean of their bed,
Behind closed doors.

We avoid this landing, using it
Only as a stepping stone from floor to floor,
A bridge from world to world,
A breath of time between imaginings.
These stairways and passages,
So dark with the regimen of rules and bedtimes
Are always leading upward to the light.
We linger only briefly,
Called to attention or to give account,
Make a promise, shake our hands in truce
Nec temere, nec timide, Suzy says,
Aware of the slipping tide but knowing
Tomorrow will always come.

3

Our third floor
Is only an inkling.
Unmapped and uninhibited,
A place of secrets and innuendo,
Where a hiding place becomes another country.
We do things differently here
And the upstairs dormitory,
Our refuge and confessional,
Is a kingdom of night-play
Where all of its citizens are angels,
Forever welcomed home.
And so, we remain in heaven.

Her footstep on the stair
Is avidly awaited
Although we flee, laughing
From the flash and snap of her fingers,
Still warm from where so recently
They clutched the banister.
We smell the splash of her perfume
As she spills through the window,
Scenting the sea-wall waves
Just on the cusp of tide-turn,
Or bursts from one of the cupboards,
Forever uncontained.

Her father, who cannot enter here,
Contents himself
To gaze at these lost worlds
From the haven of the slate bench,
Carved with flat fish along the grey sea wall,
From where his stick can divine
The slick of his girl
Although he dare not breathe her in.
Still, after all this time,
Shut out of Heaven, unmanned,
His rooms abandoned,
And wondering where she went.

4

The top floor stands in imagination only:
Her voice saved on the telephone,
The diary entry scrawl and undeciphered name,
The mysterious appointment, all a charade
Leading to nowhere games
Of consequence and murder in the dark.
And finally the trail leads only here,
To the beckoning old home
Which welcomes other families, not our own
And their legion of footsteps
On the scullery stairs
And their own treasure hunts in our back garden.

Amongst the arrivals and departures,
Amongst the muddy cases on the porch
And the skirmishes and pacts
And all the small discrepancies of childhood,
Unnoticed, she slips in and out.
You catch her drift
When all the cutlery has been laid out neatly;
An extra place at the table,
An extra crown amongst the shifting head count,
An extra sandy footprint in the hall,
A little lost girl
Who is still playing hide and seek.

THE SMELL OF TIME   *Bryn Bach*

Change, snuffed upon the water.
The house, a collected pot of smells in summer,
When neighbours call out the extermination team
Or men to dredge the drains.
There's nothing there, of course, to cause the reek,
Nothing substantial, they say,
Neither a rat's corpse nor a hunk of waste.
It is, and they shrug, just time.

The smell of time's accumulated seasons,
The scent of bacon knuckles cured on hooks,
Of one-pot stews and lava bread
And the aroma of non-conformity.
Sweet, undertones of straw from absent beds
Which folk were born and bred and died upon.
Weariness and small joys, each permeated by
The tang and singe of driftwood.

Seventeen hundred and thirty something;
That individual, final digit chipped
At the foundation hearthstone
When they moved the new boiler in.
Dates smudged at the library,
Now only open on Tuesday afternoons,
Where the creak and sigh of volunteers
Rasp amongst the empty galleries.

And down on the foreshore echoes of tribute lie,
An onion as big as a fist, escaped from crating,
Which would feed us a cawl for a week.
Sand-coated oranges from Finisterre,
And a stray fichu of lace,
Torn, like a phantom topsail by the wind
To drape across the bosoms
Of the busy mannequins of Cardigan.

At Bryn Bach there never was much
Beyond the church on the hill
And your own bed in the churchyard
Already neatly made and waiting all comfy behind.
Hard soap only tickled the water in those days,
Running a beautiful black,
Scentless and cold as marble off the mountain,
Frothing at the sharp edge of the shore.

You'll hardly recognise it now
Except in a moment of leisure, rarely earned,
Laid back on the dune, a trove of shells in hand,
Your eyes on the hurrying sky.
But there it is still, the roll and suck of water,
The cry of the ewe to her lamb,
And that smell of salt on the wood of the timber door,
As the sturdy latch clicks home.

THE RUNT OF THE LITTER   *Trenydd*

Little Trenydd, eldest of the brood,
But the runt of the litter of houses,
Stable door open-mouthed,
Windows blinking in surprise,
And wonder, even now,
Gaping at the rigmarole of the river
With each filling up
And letting out of tide.

Little Trenydd, the first built,
Squats like a baby
Counting its mothers buttons from a tin,
Cross-legged on the strand.
Soon the other houses grow around it,
Those leggy younger siblings,
Vying for height and confidence, and
Competing architectural demands.

The days have flowed to months
And years, and decades strung
On chains, like charms
Are polished to sea-shell white.
And Trenydd, forever unwilling
To let the moment pass
Without that small, astonished gasp,
Still turns its face to the light.

Tall ships give way to steam,
The fishing fleet diminished
To one peeled ferry
And then to nothing at all.
Pleasure boats and dinghies
Undignify the harbour
And, an old man now, with the sun in his eyes
Little Trenydd dozes on the wall.

CONGREGATION   *St. Mary's Church. Newport*

We gather here,
The stones at the foot of the mountain,
In thrall at last, as we have been all our lives
To its dark permanence.
Its loose flanks, mossy as a lion in moult,
The teeth still with their bite intact,
The crouch-back pounce,
Inked black against the sky,
Oh dearly beloved.

We lie in rows
Like tide breaks in the churchyard,
Our granite holds the line.
Generation by generation we make room,
Welcome our sons and daughters to the family business:
Parents and grandparents
In rows, like apples boxed up for winter.
Our ranks have formed a constellation of daisies
Where we are gathered.

And each Good Friday,
The great bells boom and shrill
And those of us that sleep here still, are shaken half awake,
To watch our dwindling faithful come,
Or an occasional passer-by, who stepped
To the foot of the mountain.
We walk with them all the way to Easter Sunday,
Then turn again to lie in our green beds,
More sleeping every year.

Oh dearly beloved.

Acknowledgements

A few of the poems have had some previous readership. *Tesserae* appeared as a text panel to accompany an exhibit at the *A Cargo of Curiosities* installation in Manchester in 2016, *In His Cups* and *The Last House on the River* were set to music and performed by Roddy Williams at the Wigmore Hall for its At Lunch season in 2014, broadcast live on BBC Radio 3 and *The Belgians* won the Foreign Voices poetry competition at Holland Park Press in 2017. The poems were always conceived as a cycle but have never appeared as a collection before.

The Author

Karen spent the early part of her working life as an actor and musician and became an ensemble member and lyricist and later artistic director of the Bristol-based theatre collective Public Parts.

From theatre she moved towards lyric and libretto writing and poetry and found herself creating verbatim texts with marginalised groups, most particularly with people living with dementia.

She has produced two anthologies of 'dementia poetry' as well as two opera libretti and a song cycle, each dealing with aspects of living with dementia, the fading of memory and the poetic language which evolves from the experience.

I Had an Angel, written with composer John O'Hara, was produced live and also as an opera film for WNO. *The Bargee's Wife*, also written with John O'Hara, was produced as a community Opera for the 3 Choirs Festival as was their song cycle *I Can Hear You Waiting*.

Most recently she created a libretto for an Oratorio with composer Thomas Johnson *The Street of Bugles* which was performed at the 3 Choirs Festival and a cycle of poetry to accompany an arts installation *A Cargo of Curiosities* with fellow writer and film-maker Chris Salt.

She was Charles Causley poet-in-residence at Cypress Well in 2016. In 2017, her poem *The Belgians* won the Foreign Voices competition.

More information is available from
http://www.hollandparkpress.co.uk/hayes

Holland Park Press is a unique publishing initiative. Its aim is to promote poetry and literary fiction, and discover new writers. It specialises in contemporary English fiction and poetry, and translations of Dutch classics. It also gives contemporary Dutch writers the opportunity to be published in Dutch and English.

To

Learn more about Karen Hayes
Discover other interesting books
Read our unique Anglo-Dutch magazine
Find out how to submit your manuscript
Take part in one of our competitions

Visit www.hollandparkpress.co.uk

Bookshop: http://www.hollandparkpress.co.uk/books.php

Holland Park Press in the social media:

http://www.twitter.com/HollandParkPres
http://www.facebook.com/HollandParkPress
http://www.linkedin.com/company/holland-park-press
http://www.youtube.com/user/HollandParkPress
http://plus.google.com/+HollandParkPress